D1433498

# FILM MUSIC

# CLASSIC *f*M
# HANDY
# GUIDES

# FILM MUSIC

ROB WEINBERG

First published 2015 by
Elliott and Thompson Limited
27 John Street
London WC1N 2BX
www.eandtbooks.com

ISBN: 978-1-78396-052-1

9 8 7 6 5 4 3 2 1

A catalogue record for this book is available from the
British Library.

Typesetting: Marie Doherty
Printed in the UK by TJ International Ltd

# Contents

# Introduction

At Classic FM, we spend a lot of our time dreaming up wonderful ways of making sure that as many people as possible across the UK have the opportunity to listen to classical music. As the nation's biggest classical music radio station, we feel that we have a responsibility to share the world's greatest music as widely as we can.

Over the years, we have written a variety of classical music books in all sorts of shapes and sizes. But we have never put together a series of books quite like this.

This set of books covers a whole range of aspects of classical music. They are all written in Classic FM's friendly, accessible style and you can rest assured that they are packed full of facts about classical music. Read separately, each book gives you a handy snapshot of a particular subject area. Added together, the series combines to offer a more detailed insight into the full story of classical music. Along the way, we shall be paying particular attention to some of the key composers whose music we play most often on the radio station, as well as examining many of classical music's subgenres.

These books are relatively small in size, so they are not going to be encyclopedic in their level of detail; there are other books out there that do that much better than we could ever hope to. Instead, they are intended to be enjoyable introductory guides that will be particularly useful to listeners who are beginning their voyage of discovery through the rich and exciting world of classical music. Drawing on the research we have undertaken for many of our previous Classic FM books, they concentrate on information rather than theory because we want to make this series of books attractive and inviting to readers who are not necessarily familiar with the more complex aspects of musicology.

For more information on this series, take a look at our website: www.ClassicFM.com/handyguides.

# Preface

If you've just picked this book up in a shop – or even already bought it – you've probably realised by now that we're on a journey to find out more about film music.

Since Classic FM's launch in 1992, we have always enjoyed making links between classical music and the movies. The first contact many of us had with the great classics – barring television commercials for Hovis or Nescafé – was when Mickey Mouse struggled to tame his wayward brooms in *Fantasia*'s 'The Sorcerer's Apprentice' sequence.

Or perhaps your first encounter with the music of Richard Wagner took place while his *Ride of the Valkyries* boomed out of Chinook helicopters thundering over Vietnam in *Apocalypse Now*?

With the invention of motion pictures, it was only to be expected that music would play a major role in accompanying the telling of stories on screen. Film was the natural evolution of the kind of storytelling for the masses pioneered by the great composers, through their operas, incidental music for theatre, and songs.

Over the past hundred years, while so-called 'serious' composers often shunned melody, beauty and harmony in their music, film composers created some of the most melodic, dramatic and inspirational orchestral music ever written. All of them were equally serious about their craft, many of them classically trained and trying to earn a living while often continuing to write for the concert hall. Many classical composers, beginning with Camille Saint-Saëns and coming up to date with Philip Glass, have created music for the big screen. Indeed it is entirely plausible to think that had Beethoven or Mozart been living in our time they would have enthusiastically embraced composing for the cinema, as they did for the theatre in their own day, and would probably be scoring video games as well, a genre in which a number of today's most successful film composers have cut their teeth.

Classic FM proudly showcases film music every day in its shows, specifically *Saturday Night at the Movies* every weekend, featuring the greatest scores, exciting new releases and the world's favourite classical pieces as heard in the movies.

For a genre that is just one century old, it is remarkable that so many film themes have rapidly become loved the world over, with a life of their own outside the cinema – in the concert hall and on albums. The majority of music lovers would not hesitate to call the themes to *Schindler's List* or *Lawrence of Arabia* classics.

So we shall make no apology to the classical purists for giving film music the credit and exposure it deserves. It not only contributes to a great experience at the cinema – boosting the excitement and enhancing emotions – but also opens the world of great orchestral and choral music to the biggest imaginable audience.

*one*

# Pioneering Days

It might seem ironic to begin the story of film music with an era when movies had no sound, but cinema's love affair with music dates right back to the era before the 'talkies' arrived. Today, silent-movie buffs even argue that this was the real golden age, when the score was foreground – not background – music, played live in the movie theatre. In those days composers didn't have to fight to have their work heard over ear-bursting sound effects and dialogue.

As early as the 1890s, some short films might have had a pianist sitting in front of the screen tinkling along to the pictures; certainly, in December 1895, the Lumière family was testing out some of its films in Paris with a piano accompaniment.

By the following year, several London venues were screening films alongside a full orchestra. But it's also possible that the music was there for a very practical purpose – to drown out the clanking of the projector, or to keep the audience happy while the film was being rewound or new spools were loaded up.

In those days little thought was given to matching what was being played with what was happening up on the screen, as pianists hammered their way through a selection of irrelevant ragtime tunes. But as cinema audiences became more sophisticated, they demanded more from the music that went with the experience. Film companies began sending out 'cue sheets' with the reels, listing the major scenes of the film, their duration, and suggestions for appropriate pieces of music – often classical ones – to be performed. Very often, whole extracts were lifted from the works of Beethoven and Tchaikovsky. But even as early as 1904, the operetta composer and conductor Herman Finck (1872–1939) was employed as a music director in London, writing accompanying music to films, as well as editing selections of classical favourites to be performed by orchestras in cinemas.

It was only a few years before classical composers were approached to create scores for movies. Frenchman Camille Saint-Saëns (1835–1921) was probably the first big name to provide one. In 1908, he wrote the music for the eighteen-minute-long *L'Assassinat du Duc de Guise*. Its producers – who had also encouraged well-known stage actors to perform in their films to give them some kudos – made a big deal about promoting the fact that Saint-Saëns had provided music for their movie.

In 1913, a former pupil of the Czech composer Antonín Dvořák, John Stepan Zamecnik (1872–1953), published the first widely distributed sheet music for silent film accompaniment. The volume, titled *Sam Fox Moving Picture Music, Volume 1*, consisted of twenty-five piano pieces, covering the most essential backing music for comedies and melodramas. The book and its sequels remained bestsellers throughout the silent era.

Sadly, most of the composers of the period are now forgotten; they received no credit for their compositions, their music was never recorded and then, to cap it all, the medium they were working in died with the coming of sound.

## Charles Chaplin (1889–1977)

One enduring figure from the era – the first global superstar – was Charles Chaplin. He not only directed, scripted and produced but also wrote the music for his own films. Claude Debussy, no less, sought out Chaplin in Paris and told him he was 'instinctively a musician and a dancer'. Among the other composers that Chaplin numbered among his friends were Sergei Rachmaninov, Igor Stravinsky and Arnold Schoenberg. But Chaplin had no formal training in either reading or writing music; he resorted to singing his tunes for others to write down.

## Carl Davis (born in 1936)

A modern composer whose contribution to providing scores for silent movies is second to none is Carl Davis. Since 1980, when Channel 4 television began broadcasting a series of restored prints of classic films, Davis has created magnificent music for more than fifty of them. In 1983, after a Paris screening of Abel Gance's epic *Napoléon* (1927), Davis was honoured with the order of Chevalier des Arts et des Lettres. Live performances of silent classics with Davis scores have become a fixture of cinemas around the world.

Ever since motion pictures began, experiments had been going on to try to match film to recorded music. As early as 1900, short films were screened with an orchestral score played from a disc. Warner Brothers put together a disc of music played by the New York Philharmonic – complete with sound effects – to play alongside the premiere of *Don Juan* (1926), starring John Barrymore. In 1925, the Phonofilm system introduced the idea of recording a soundtrack on a narrow strip down the side of the film. Then, in 1927, there was great excitement when a Fox newsreel showing Charles Lindbergh's non-stop flight from New York to Paris included sound. In October of that year, *The Jazz Singer*, starring Al Jolson, changed everything. The public went mad for the film's four sound segments, and studios accelerated their move to sound film production. It would take an Austrian-born immigrant to take movie music to its next stage – what has been called the Golden Age of Hollywood film scores.

*two*

# The Golden Age

The so-called Golden Age of Hollywood film music – all swashbuckling adventures, *film noir* thrillers and sweeping romances – really was launched by a giant monkey. *King Kong* (1933) heralded a new era in which the score became an ever more important part of the cinema experience.

**Max Steiner (1888–1971)**

*King Kong* helped to establish the reputation of the 'father of film music', Max Steiner, one of the most brilliant of all movie composers. Born in Vienna, Steiner was a child prodigy who had studied with Johannes Brahms and Gustav Mahler and counted Richard Strauss as his godfather. By the time he was twenty, Steiner was earning a living as a conductor and theatre composer. He left Austria for Britain and then the United States, working as an orchestrator and conductor on Broadway for eleven years.

Steiner arrived in Hollywood just as the major studios were embracing sound and wrote the first fully integrated score – for *Symphony of Six Million* (1932) – revolutionising the movie industry's approach to music. For *King Kong*, his grand symphonic score, particularly the use of a three-note musical motif depicting the beast, set the standard for everything that was to follow. Steiner made extensive use of the *leitmotif* – a technique favoured by Wagner in which musical phrases are linked to particular characters and heard even when the character is not visible on screen to evoke him or her in the viewer's memory.

*King Kong* also introduced the idea of giving a film an overture and exit music, previewing – or, at the end, reprising – the score's main themes.

### Erich Wolfgang Korngold (1897–1957)

Another former child prodigy from Central Europe who set a high standard for film scoring was Erich Wolfgang Korngold. The composer of only sixteen soundtracks, it is for his music for Errol

Flynn's adventure pictures that Korngold is best remembered.

Korngold wrote his first orchestral music as a teenager and, like Steiner, also won adulation from the likes of Richard Strauss. Mahler described the young Erich as a 'musical genius'. Korngold wrote chamber music, a piano concerto and four operas, including the haunting *Die tote Stadt* (1919). In 1934, Korngold was invited to Hollywood to arrange Felix Mendelssohn's music for a star-studded production of *A Midsummer Night's Dream*. The following year, the composer signed a contract with Warner Brothers. *Captain Blood* (1935) properly launched both his and Errol Flynn's careers. Korngold continued to mix film work with concert pieces until Hitler annexed Austria. Then, the composer moved his family to the US and concentrated exclusively on film scores, vowing not to write concert works again until Hitler fell.

Combining huge skill and intelligence, Korngold's film music is bold, brassy, exciting and, at times, heart-wrenchingly romantic. Korngold had an instinctive sense of what worked dramatically and musically, based on his experience working in the theatre in Vienna. He often took the liberty of telling a producer where a scene should go or even asked for more footage to extend a scene to fit his music. His 1938 Academy Award for his score to *The Adventures of Robin Hood* marked the first time that an Oscar was awarded to a single composer rather than the head of the studio music department.

After the Second World War, with swashbucklers out of fashion, Korngold returned to Europe to resume his concert music career but sadly found himself forgotten in his homeland.

### Alfred Newman (1901–1970)

Alfred Newman was not only a great film composer, he also wielded more power than any of his contemporaries. Formerly a Broadway conductor, Newman travelled to Hollywood with the songwriter Irving Berlin and had private lessons with Arnold Schoenberg.

As head of music at 20th Century Fox for two decades, Newman pioneered a method of synchronising the film with the recording and performance of its score, known as the 'Newman System', which is still in use today. He scored more than 250 pictures, the best of which were for portentous religious epics, replete with heavenly choirs and shimmering strings. His score for *The Song of Bernadette* (1943) became one of the first actual film scores to be released on disc, rather than its music being re-recorded for commercial release. Newman was also responsible for the 20th Century Fox fanfare – now best known as the prelude to the *Star Wars* theme tune.

Newman also spawned a dynasty of film composers – his brothers Emil and Lionel were also in the business, and his sons David and Thomas are both successful composers today, as is his nephew Randy.

## Hugo Friedhofer (1901–1981)

Before finding himself in great demand as an orchestrator and composer, Hugo Friedhofer started life accompanying silent films and stage shows. He was brought to the attention of Korngold and hired by Warner Brothers to arrange and orchestrate scores for both Steiner and Korngold.

Friedhofer worked uncredited on more than 120 films before receiving his first full composing credit for *The Adventures of Marco Polo* (1938). When he finally broke free of anonymity and arranging other people's music, he hit the jackpot with *The Best Years of Our Lives* (1946), a touching score that won him an Oscar. With some 250 films to his name, Friedhofer is only now becoming more appreciated as one of Hollywood's great composers.

## Franz Waxman (1906–1967)

Another refugee from Nazi-occupied Europe who found his way to Hollywood and studied with Schoenberg in Los Angeles was Franz Waxman. Almost immediately he struck gold with his strange and haunting score for *The Bride of Frankenstein* (1935). Universal Studios offered Waxman a two-year contract as music director, scoring more than twenty films a year, after which he moved on to MGM, Warner Brothers and Paramount. He won two Oscars for *Sunset Boulevard* (1950) and *A Place in the Sun* (1951).

## Miklós Rózsa (1907–1995)

Hungarian Miklós Rózsa was a graduate of the Leipzig Conservatory and his concert works were performed in Paris. Moving to London, his fellow countryman Alexander Korda commissioned him to start composing for films. Rózsa relocated to

California to complete *The Thief of Baghdad* (1940) and remained there for the rest of his life.

Rózsa composed music for more than a hundred films, winning three Oscars and a further fourteen nominations. His style ranges from the stridently epic and rich romanticism of *Ben-Hur* (1959) to eerie *film noir* scores. *Spellbound* (1945), for Alfred Hitchcock, employs the early electronic instrument, the theremin. Rózsa later adapted his score into a concert piece, the *Spellbound Concerto*.

### Bernard Herrmann (1911–1975)

Bernard Herrmann owed his lucky break to Orson Welles, with whom he worked in radio. Welles commissioned Herrmann to provide the score for his first film – and masterpiece – *Citizen Kane* (1941). In his music for *Kane*, Herrmann demonstrated that he could successfully tackle any style of music – from grand opera to jaunty humour. Later he would apply his considerable talent to every genre, ranging from psychological thrillers to 'sword-and-sorcery' adventures.

In later years, when the director Steven Spielberg was expressing his admiration to Herrmann, the composer – famous for his irascibility – retorted,

'If ya admire my music so much, why do ya always use Johnny Williams for your pictures?'

But it is for his collaboration with Alfred Hitchcock that Herrmann is best remembered; he was the master of the dark, brooding atmosphere. In *Psycho* (1960), his screeching violins for the shower scene have inspired horror-movie soundtracks to this day.

## David Raksin (1912–2004)

The commercial power of putting a good melody in a movie was first noticed properly when Fox Studios were inundated with requests after *Laura* (1944). After Newman and Herrmann separately refused to score it, David Raksin's theme became a huge hit with five different versions making it into the US Top 10. During Raksin's own lifetime, *'Laura'* was said to be the second most recorded song ever.

Raksin – who lived into his nineties and became known as the 'grandfather of film music' – had worked with Charles Chaplin on *Modern Times* (1936), with Chaplin thinking up the tunes and Raksin writing them down. Raksin was Oscar-nominated for both *Forever Amber* (1947) and *Separate Tables* (1958).

Most of Hollywood's Golden Age composers continued to work beyond the decade of the 1940s but, particularly thanks to Herrmann, film music broke free from its Romantic European classical roots and become something altogether more individual, more supportive of the story – and less overwhelming.

Yet the style of the giants of the Golden Age has left its mark, particularly on the magnificent soundtracks of John Williams. Think *Star Wars*, *Indiana Jones*, *Schindler's List* – and you'll realise the Golden Age never really ended.

# three

# New Directions

The 1950s signalled an era of innovation and experimentation in cinema. As television began to emerge as the decade's dominant form of entertainment, film-makers had to employ the latest technology to make things bigger and better to keep the punters coming in.

Epic movies still required the likes of Alfred Newman and Miklós Rózsa to do what they did best, but a revolution in the music industry at the end of the 1940s – the introduction of the long-playing record and the 7-inch single – resulted in a change of attitude towards film. The *'Harry Lime Theme'* by Anton Karas from *The Third Man* (1949) stayed at the top of the charts for almost three months in 1950. This typically mid-European tune, played on a zither by an unknown performer, pioneered a new kind of musical authenticity in film scoring and demonstrated that studios were willing to move away from the grand romantic score into other kinds of music for film. The rock'n'roll revolution also began to make an impact when Bill Haley's 'Rock Around The Clock' was used as the theme for *The Blackboard Jungle* (1955).

## Dimitri Tiomkin (1894–1979)

The value of using music to generate advance excitement about a movie was also recognised when the song 'Do Not Forsake Me, O My Darlin'', an integral part of *High Noon* (1952), became a hit and served to promote the film. The formula was repeated by its composer Dimitri Tiomkin with *Friendly Persuasion* (1956) and the song 'Thee I Love'.

Tiomkin was a Ukrainian pianist who had given the 1928 European premiere in Paris of George Gershwin's Piano Concerto. Tiomkin's breakthrough as a composer came with *Lost Horizon* (1937) and its quasi-mystical sound world of chanting and percussion. Ironically, for a Russian, Tiomkin made his biggest mark on that most American of genres

– the Western – with his expansive, folk-tinged scores. His triumphant music for *The Fall of the Roman Empire* (1964) is as big as Hollywood epic soundtracks ever got.

### Georges Auric (1899–1983)

In Britain, Ealing Studios employed Georges Auric to bring wit and elegance to their distinctive comedies. Auric was among the most outstanding composers of film music. Originally he was a member of Les Six, a circle of French composers who had gathered around the poet-playwright Jean Cocteau to produce a simple and vibrant form of French music. Cocteau was keen to expand his cultural vision into film and began his collaboration with Auric on the imaginative *La Belle et la bête* (1946). In addition to the work Auric produced for Ealing, he also scored a number of Hollywood romantic comedies, including *Roman Holiday* (1953).

### Alex North (1910–1991)

With Alex North's score to *A Streetcar Named Desire* (1951), jazz entered the vocabulary of film composers and movie music found a distinctly American voice. North had studied composition with Aaron Copland and wrote ballet scores and music for the theatre. His thrilling music for *Spartacus* (1960) is one of cinema's greatest epic soundtracks. It's a richly varied, inventively orchestrated score, shifting from the brassy and percussive to tender romanticism. North also had a huge international hit with his theme for *Unchained* (1955), better known as 'Unchained Melody', which was later revived for *Ghost* (1990).

### Jerome Moross (1913–1983)

A former school friend of Bernard Herrmann, Moross began his career in Hollywood as an orchestrator before establishing his name as a film composer with another blockbusting Western, *The Big Country* (1958). Moross's first film scores for low-budget movies earned him sufficient money to fund his other career as a composer for the concert hall. With *The Big Country*, he perfected a rugged, expansive style that perfectly conjured up images of the American plains. In spite of considerable success, Moross saw his work for the movies as being of secondary importance to his 'serious' compositions.

## Elmer Bernstein (1922–2004)

The introduction of jazz into film scores also launched the career of Elmer Bernstein, one of Hollywood's greatest masters of movie music. Bernstein's sparse, lyrical jazz score for *The Man with the Golden Arm* (1955) demonstrated to producers the commercial value of recouping a movie's costs with a popular record. His rollicking *The Magnificent Seven* (1960) theme and *The Great Escape* (1963), with its cheery march, both became classics that have enjoyed a long, independent life in the concert hall, on recordings and as favourites for military bands. Bernstein also became a champion of a pioneering electronic instrument, the Ondes martenot, which he used in several of his scores.

Throughout cinema's brief history, the retelling of classic stories – be they biblical, mythological or great works of literature – progressed side by side with filmmakers' reflecting on the concerns and issues of their own times. If the 1950s was a decade of youthful rebellion and challenging the past, the 1960s saw Hollywood entering its jet-set era, opening up to a whole world of influences and styles.

*four*

# Expanding Horizons

Cinemagoers' horizons in the late 1950s and early 1960s were expanded to accommodate the so-called 'new wave' of films emerging from France. Of all the French composers who emerged in the 1960s, Maurice Jarre created the scores that are the most internationally recognisable and enduring.

### Maurice Jarre (1924–2009)

Throughout the 1950s, Jarre collaborated with the director Georges Franju, writing a number of avant-garde soundtracks. Jarre's breakthrough came when he was approached to compose the music to David Lean's epic *Lawrence of Arabia* (1962) after the director's attempts to sign up Malcolm Arnold,

William Walton, Benjamin Britten and Aram Khachaturian all failed. Jarre completed the magnificent music in just four weeks and won himself an Oscar. A legendary partnership with Lean was born, which resulted in Jarre winning further Academy Awards for *Dr Zhivago* (1965) and *A Passage to India* (1984).

## Nino Rota (1911–1979)

Emerging from Italy, Nino Rota became one of the most prolific of all film composers with almost 150 scores to his name, as well as ballets, operas, choral and chamber works. The composer's long-standing partnership with the director Federico Fellini began with *The White Sheik* (1952) and continued through to Fellini's last film, *Orchestra Rehearsal* (1978). Fellini said of Rota, 'He was someone who had a rare quality belonging to the world of intuition. Just like children, simple men, sensitive people, innocent people, he would suddenly say dazzling things. As soon as he arrived, stress disappeared, everything turned into a festive atmosphere; the movie entered a joyful, serene, fantastic period, a new life.'

Rota's theme from Zeffirelli's *Romeo and Juliet* (1968) became a number one hit and was heard daily on British radio for more than a decade when Simon Bates used it to underscore his weekday *Our Tune* feature. His most famous work is the traditional-style score he composed for *The Godfather* (1972). Its love theme, with lyrics added, became the worldwide hit, *'Speak Softly Love'*. Rota won an Oscar for its sequel, *The Godfather Part II* (1974).

**Ennio Morricone (born in 1928)**

Another Italian movie-music legend emerged in the 1960s and has continued to produce masterful scores into the twenty-first century. Ennio Morricone has always considered himself a composer of concert music who writes for films 'on the side'. Yet his extensive, magnificent output has placed him firmly in the pantheon of great film composers. Morricone's name will forever be linked with the director Sergio Leone, with whom he first collaborated on *A Fistful of Dollars* (1964) – a film that reinvented the Western genre – and subsequent 'Spaghetti Westerns'. Morricone's sound palette of coyote howls, whistles, whips, harmonicas, electric guitars and lyric-free vocals established him as a true original of film music.

## Jerry Goldsmith (1929–2004)

One of Hollywood's all-time masters of movie music emerged in the 1960s and continued on magnificent form for four decades. Jerry Goldsmith attended classes given by Miklós Rózsa at the University of Southern California before getting work as a clerk in the music department of CBS. Composing work for television and radio dramas followed, where Goldsmith built his reputation providing the music for series including *Gunsmoke* and *The Twilight Zone*. His compositions – which spanned every kind of genre – often showed off an adventurous spirit, one willing to experiment with unusual sounds and technology. In his music for *Planet of the Apes* (1968), Goldsmith incorporated all manner of percussion including household utensils and ram's horns. He won his only Oscar for the sinister, choral soundtrack for *The Omen* (1976).

## Henry Mancini (1924–1994)

One of the most successful and influential film composers of the 1960s, Henry Mancini never worked in the grand symphonic style. Much of his music is quintessentially of its time – swinging, light and frivolous. The popularity of the ballad *'Moon River'* from *Breakfast at Tiffany's* (1961) meant that Mancini was expected to deliver chart hits alongside every one of his scores. He paved the way for the likes of Lalo Schifrin, Burt Bacharach and John Barry to create film music that was stylistically inseparable from the pop styles of the day.

## John Barry (1933–2011)

Barry started out with his own jazz combo – the John Barry Seven – working closely with teen idol Adam Faith. Barry was asked to arrange the music for Faith's first film, *Beat Girl* (1960) before working on James Bond's first outing, *Dr No* (1962). Ten Bond scores by Barry followed in which he made his indelible mark on the series' sound. Although the original James Bond theme was written by Monty Norman, Barry's Bond songs resulted in numerous chart hits, as did his Oscar-winning *Born Free* (1966) score. More awards followed for *The Lion in Winter* (1968), *Out of Africa* (1985) and *Dances with Wolves* (1990). In the main themes for the latter two, Barry reached the peak of his powers, demonstrating his enduring gift for sweeping, romantic melodies.

The 1960s and 1970s were also the decades in which directors increasingly incorporated classical music into their soundtracks, bringing works to worldwide audiences that up until then had been enjoyed mainly by concertgoers.

The Swedish film *Elvira Madigan* (1967) granted Mozart's Piano Concerto No. 21 a new lease of life and a subtitle by which it has been known ever since. The release of *2001: A Space Odyssey* (1968), coinciding with the global excitement at America's and Russia's space programmes, made the '*Sunrise*' opening to Richard Strauss's *Also Sprach Zarathustra* an often heard anthem for the space age, as well as for grand sporting occasions. *2001*'s director Stanley Kubrick would later also turn to works from the classical repertoire in his soundtrack choices for other films, including *A Clockwork Orange* (1971) and *The Shining* (1980).

Luchino Visconti's languorous adaptation of *Death in Venice* (1971), starring Dirk Bogarde as a dying composer – loosely based on Mahler – made exceptional use of the heart-rending *Adagietto* movement of Mahler's own *Symphony No. 5*.

*five*

# New Frontiers

Orchestral film music at the beginning of the 1970s was in the doldrums. It was American urban funk music that made the biggest impact on the soundtracks of the era with Isaac Hayes' *Shaft*, the precursor to disco domination towards the end of the decade with the huge success of *Saturday Night Fever* (1977). Throughout the early 1970s, Jerry Goldsmith kept the flag flying for the composed, original score and delivered superlative soundtracks for the likes of *The Mephisto Waltz* (1971), *Tora! Tora! Tora!* (1970) and *The Other* (1972).

It was thanks, however, to the public's seem-ingly insatiable appetite for disaster movies that a talent emerged mid-decade – John Williams, who went on to become the most successful movie composer of all time.

### John Williams (born in 1932)

John Williams trained as a concert pianist before conducting bands in the US Air Force. He took composition lessons from Mario Castelnuovo-Tedesco, who also taught Jerry Goldsmith. As a pianist, Williams worked for Alfred Newman and Franz Waxman – and provided the famous walking-bass piano riff for Henry Mancini's *Peter Gunn* television theme – before taking up composing for series including *Wagon Train* and *Lost in Space*. The demands of delivering up to one hour of music a week honed his craft as a composer, although his first Oscar was awarded for his adaptation of the stage show *Fiddler on the Roof* (1971). High-profile work on disaster movies followed, including *Earthquake* (1974), *The Poseidon Adventure* (1972) and *The Towering Inferno* (1974).

Williams' collaboration with director Steven Spielberg began with *The Sugarland Express* (1974). Their partnership has given the world not only some of its biggest box-office smashes, but some of the best-loved film themes of all time – music that exists in its own right outside the films as favourites in the concert hall, on albums and on Classic FM.

*Star Wars* (1977) – all brassy fanfares and Holst-style marches – was the one soundtrack that single-handedly revived the tradition of the big orchestral film score. On disc, it became the biggest-selling non-pop record ever. Along with *Raiders of the Lost Ark* (1981) and *Superman* (1978), it recalls the Golden Age of Korngold, Rózsa and Steiner. For *Schindler's List* (1993), *Jurassic Park* (1993), *Born on the Fourth of July* (1989) and *Saving Private Ryan* (1998), Williams penned some of the most emotionally stirring orchestral music of the late twentieth century.

John Williams is the most Oscar-nominated person ever – and with more music on its way for the resumption of the *Star Wars* franchise, it seems that the octogenarian movie-music genius is simply unstoppable.

### Vangelis (born in 1943)

While John Williams and the spate of *Star Wars*-spawned sci-fi blockbusters revived film music's grand orchestral tradition, the Greek musician

Evangelos Odysseas Papathanassiou, known as Vangelis, was revolutionising the use of electronics on soundtracks. For *Chariots of Fire* (1981), a period drama about British Olympic athletes, Vangelis' brand of synthesizer-generated music was an unusual choice. But the gamble paid off – *Chariots* was a runaway international hit, as a film and a soundtrack, and Vangelis went on to provide atmospheric scores for numerous other films including the futuristic cult classic *Blade Runner* (1982).

### James Horner (born in 1953)

James Horner hit gold with the second big-screen outing for Captain Kirk and the crew of the USS *Enterprise*, *Star Trek II: The Wrath of Khan* (1982). American-born – but educated at London's Royal College of Music – Horner set out to be an avant-garde composer for the concert hall but soon caught the film-music bug, writing for science-fiction B-movies.

Horner was nominated for an Oscar for *Aliens* (1986), directed by James Cameron, and the two reunited for *Titanic* (1997), leading to a global phenomenon and a smash-hit single, *'My Heart*

*Will Go On'*. Horner's scores – including *Braveheart* (1995) and *Titanic* – have often made use of unusual traditional instruments, such as bagpipes and whistles. He continues to compose evocative scores, though nothing has topped his blockbusting form of the late 1990s. For *Troy* (2004), Horner stepped in a few weeks before the film's premiere when the director decided to ditch the music that Gabriel Yared, composer of *The English Patient* (1996), had spent a year working on. In a month, Horner produced a magnificent epic score that recalls the best of Rózsa and Korngold.

**Michael Kamen (1948–2003)**

A fluency in both pop and classical styles characterised the music of Michael Kamen. His résumé reads like a roll-call of pop royalty: he worked with Kate Bush, the Eurythmics, Pink Floyd, Bob Dylan and Eric Clapton, to name but a few. Kamen's first major film assignment was scoring David Cronenberg's *The Dead Zone* (1983). Working with *Monty Python*'s Terry Gilliam on *Brazil* (1985) brought out the best in the composer – his soundtrack is one of the movie-music masterpieces of the 1980s. His Bryan Adams-sung theme for

*Robin Hood, Prince of Thieves* (1991), '*Everything I Do*', topped the UK charts for a staggering sixteen weeks in 1991, demonstrating the power of a good film tune to generate audiences, revenue and excitement about going to the cinema.

*six*

# Into the New Century

A t the end of the 1980s, one composer emerged on the movie scene whose sound – and influence – dominated film music for the 1990s and continues to do so into the second decade of the twenty-first century.

### Hans Zimmer (born in 1957)

Just as Hollywood's composers of the 1950s brought jazz into the vocabulary of film music, Hans Zimmer has successfully blended conventional orchestral and choral forces with rock elements – including synthesizers and electronic drums – to create a thrilling, contemporary sound.

The German-born composer began his musical career working with rock bands including the

Damned, Ultravox and the Buggles. As an apprentice to English film composer Stanley Myers, Zimmer provided music for a number of movies in the mid-1980s including *My Beautiful Laundrette* (1985) starring Daniel Day-Lewis.

Zimmer's big break came with an invitation from director Barry Levinson to score *Rain Man* (1988), starring Tom Cruise and Dustin Hoffman. His soundtrack to Ridley Scott's *Black Rain* (1989) was a particular milestone, featuring the composer's now familiar mix of computer-generated sounds, electronic percussion and orchestra and casting the mould for almost every action feature in the decade to follow. Zimmer won his first Oscar for Disney's *The Lion King* (1994), in which he seamlessly blended large orchestral forces with the African choral music of Lebo M and Elton John's songs. His collaboration with Lisa Gerrard on Ridley Scott's *Gladiator* (2000) gave Zimmer a worldwide, bestselling album. The composer and the director have also worked together on *Thelma and Louise* (1991), *Black Hawk Down* (2001), *Hannibal* (2001) and *Matchstick Men* (2003).

The partnership between Ridley Scott and Hans Zimmer – and more recently the director

Christopher Nolan with Zimmer – continues the tradition in which directors and composers can enjoy a particularly successful working collaboration: think Hitchcock and Herrmann, Lean and Jarre, Fellini and Rota, Spielberg and Williams. This close partnership – which often brings out the best in both – has continued in recent times with a number of highly creative pairings.

## Howard Shore (born in 1946)

Howard Shore owes his initial success to the Canadian master of shock horror, David Cronenberg, and his worldwide fame to New Zealand's very own *Lord of the Rings* director Peter Jackson.

Born in Toronto, Shore toured with rock bands and wrote incidental music for theatre and radio before landing the music director's job on US television's *Saturday Night Live*. His collaboration with Cronenberg began with *The Brood* (1979) and has continued for thirty years, up to and including Cronenberg's more recent, mainstream – but equally bloody – thrillers. For Cronenberg, Shore provided one of his grandest early achievements, *The Fly* (1986), which the composer later turned into an opera that has been staged in Paris and the US.

The three monumental *Lord of the Rings* soundtracks firmly established Shore as an A-list Hollywood composer and dominated the album charts around the world. A foretaste of his talent for marshalling orchestral and choral elements can be heard in his exquisite score for Al Pacino's *Looking for Richard* (1996). For *Lord of the Rings*, the composer pulled out all the stops, brought in world-class soloists and singers and created a contemporary classical masterpiece, now performed to sold-out concert halls. He has returned to Middle Earth during this present decade with Peter Jackson's *The Hobbit* trilogy.

### Danny Elfman (born in 1949)

Another distinctive and devoted partnership is the one enjoyed by the maverick director Tim Burton and composer Danny Elfman.

Burton first encountered the composer playing with his rock band, Oingo Boingo. The two discovered they had a natural chemistry and between them created a trademark fantasy world with Elfman's offbeat, manic, musical wit and swirling fairy-tale orchestration a perfect match for Burton's skewed artistic vision. Their partnership gave the superhero genre an unusual twist with *Batman* (1989) and *Batman Returns* (1992) and has continued with quirky remakes of *Sleepy Hollow* (1999), *Charlie and the Chocolate Factory* (2005) and *Alice in Wonderland* (2010). Elfman's most universally familiar work to date, however, has been for the small screen – the theme tune to *The Simpsons*.

## Thomas Newman (born in 1955)

The influence of film legend Alfred Newman continues into our own time with his sons Thomas and David, and nephew Randy, all enjoying successful careers as movie composers and making their mark on modern-day Hollywood. Thomas Newman's music seems to flit between two styles – a quintessentially American symphonic sentimentality, as in *Little Women* (1994), and a sparse, chilling minimalist approach with reverberating piano and strange percussion, as heard on *American Beauty* (1999). The latter has been influential on Hollywood's younger composers and has even translated well into Pixar animated features.

## James Newton Howard (born in 1951)

Classically trained James Newton Howard moved

into movies after years as a session musician, pianist, producer and arranger for the likes of Elton John, Cher and Chaka Khan. The composer has enjoyed a strong director–composer relationship with M. Night Shyamalan for whom he has created bleak, Herrmannesque soundtracks for several films, including *The Sixth Sense* (1999). Howard's collaborations with Hans Zimmer on the rebooted *Batman* franchise are among his best work.

## Elliot Goldenthal (born in 1954)

Elliot Goldenthal's soundtracks are characterised by a symphonic weight that reveals his classical music roots. He first came to the public's attention with the music he composed for the third film in the *Alien* franchise, *Alien³* (1992), followed by the sweeping gothic romanticism of *Interview with the Vampire* (1994). His Oscar-winning soundtrack for *Frida* (2002) was an immaculately produced, Latin-style guitar score.

## Mychael Danna (born in 1958)

Having been exposed to both Early and World Music while studying in Toronto, the Canadian Mychael Danna has created highly sophisticated film scores that evocatively blend non-Western traditions with orchestral and electronic music. After collaborating with director Ang Lee on *The Ice Storm* (1997) and *Ride with the Devil* (1999), Danna created a richly inventive soundtrack for Lee's *Life of Pi* (2012), which won the composer his first Oscar.

### Michael Giacchino (born in 1967)

Michael Giacchino is perhaps the most talented younger composer who has made it onto Hollywood's movie-composer A-list in recent years. He emerged from writing music for video games to composing for TV, scoring shows including *Lost* (2004) for the director J. J. Abrams. Its music uniquely employed spare pieces of a plane fuselage for percussion parts, and was described by *The New Yorker*'s celebrated critic Alex Ross as 'some of the most compelling film music of the past year'. That same year, Giacchino received his first big feature-film commission for Pixar's *The Incredibles* (2004). He went on to score the Abrams-directed *Mission: Impossible III* (2006) and Disney–Pixar's *Ratatouille* (2007), for which he received his first Academy Award nomination. He has continued to work with Disney–Pixar on *Up* (2009) – which won him his first Oscar – and collaborated with Abrams again on the new *Star Trek* series (2009–2013).

### Patrick Doyle (born in 1953)

In Britain, Scottish composer Patrick Doyle enjoyed the unique position of being part of the repertory company of creative talents that put Kenneth Branagh, Emma Thompson and their friends at the forefront of British theatre and cinema in the 1990s. Doyle's score for Branagh's *Henry V* (1989) – featuring the stirring chorus *'Non Nobis Domine'* – was a triumph. The later life-affirming score for *Much Ado About Nothing* (1993) is one of the finest of the 1990s. Doyle's pastiche Mozartian music for Emma Thompson's production of *Sense and Sensibility* (1995) enjoyed a long run in the Classic FM chart in the mid-1990s.

### David Arnold (born in 1962)

Another British composer who has successfully cracked Hollywood is Luton-born David Arnold. His big break on the sci-fi film *Stargate* (1994) led to the over-the-top bombast of *Independence Day* (1996) and Arnold taking on John Barry's mantle as James Bond's composer-in-residence. Starting with

*Tomorrow Never Dies* (1997), Arnold has scored five Bond outings and made the sound his own – building on Barry's legacy and introducing elements of rock, drum-and-bass and high-tech pyrotechnics into his highly accomplished soundtracks.

## Steven Price (born in 1977)

A most promising movie-music hope who has emerged from Britain recently is Steven Price. A guitarist from the age of five, Price contributed string arrangements, and played on albums alongside rock musicians such as Michael Hutchence and U2's Bono. He went on to work as a programmer, arranger and performer with film-music composer Trevor Jones and as music editor for Howard Shore on *The Lord of the Rings* trilogy. In 2013, Price composed the highly original score for Alfonso Cuarón's *Gravity*, for which he won the Academy Award for Best Original Score.

## Ryuichi Sakamoto (born in 1952)

Synthesizer wizard Ryuichi Sakamoto was a founding member of the Japanese electronic pop group Yellow Magic Orchestra. He not only scored *Merry Christmas, Mr Lawrence* (1983), but also starred in it alongside David Bowie. Its catchy oriental theme became a chart hit as *'Forbidden Colours'*, sung by David Sylvian. Sakamoto received an Oscar with Talking Heads' frontman David Byrne for Bertolucci's epic, *The Last Emperor* (1987). He has produced atmospheric, piano-based scores for a number of Japanese films as well as contributing to the Oscar-winning soundtrack for *Babel* (2007).

## Alexandre Desplat (born in 1961)

Born to a French father and a Greek mother, Alexandre Desplat has composed extensively for French cinema and Hollywood, writing music for more than a hundred films. He has received six Academy Award nominations and provided superb scores for such as films as *The Queen* (2006), *The Curious Case of Benjamin Button* (2008), *Harry Potter and the Deathly Hallows* (2010/11) and *The King's Speech* (2011).

## Gustavo Santaolalla (born in 1951)

An Argentinian who has become one of the most in-demand composers in Hollywood is Gustavo Santaolalla. His music for *Brokeback Mountain* (2005) beat off strong competition – including two John Williams scores – to win the 2005 Oscar. Santaolalla's success was consolidated the following year when he took another Best Original Score Oscar for *Babel* (2006).

### Dario Marianelli (born in 1963)

Another international composer who has made an impact on contemporary movie music is Dario Marianelli. The Italian's star rose quickly after he scored the Keira Knightley version of *Pride and Prejudice* (2005), featuring exquisite piano music performed by the French pianist Jean-Yves Thibaudet. *Atonement* (2007), also featuring Thibaudet, and also starring Knightley, took the Oscar in 2007.

In recent years, women composers have made inroads into the male movie-music stronghold as well: **Debbie Wiseman** (born in 1963), whose bittersweet score for *Wilde* (1997) evoked the trials of the Victorian era's most controversial aesthete; **Rachel Portman** (born in 1960) who won an Oscar in 1996 for *Emma*; and **Anne Dudley** (born in 1956), whose soundtrack for *The Full Monty* (1997) picked up an Academy Award the following year.

The arrival on the movie scene in recent years of talented composers from various parts of the world, effortlessly bringing to film scores an understanding of many diverse genres of music, bodes well for the future of movie music, an art form that is still barely a century old.

As John Williams has said, 'The process has really only begun. What's happened in the last five or six decades has only been setting up a preparation, and a keen interest, and an awareness of the great musical opportunity that's here. It's an art form that's in its infancy. That's what's exciting.'

# seven

# Classical Composers at the Movies

As we learned at the beginning of this book, some of cinema's earliest pioneers were eager to get composers involved in writing music for the screen, and it was Saint-Saëns who, in 1908, was commissioned to write the music for *L'Assassinat du duc de Guise*. Maybe because of the considerable expense added to the budget of a film by hiring a classical composer to provide a score, the idea didn't take off immediately. But by the late 1920s and the arrival of sound films, composers were not only in great demand, they relished the opportunity to earn much-needed cash from providing music for the movies.

### Dmitri Shostakovich (1906–1975)

In Russia, the young Dmitri Shostakovich worked as an improvising pianist in the cinema, although he was sacked for laughing so much during one comedy that he forgot to continue playing. In 1929, he was commissioned to write the score for *The New Babylon* and pioneered the music for Russia's first sound films. Shostakovich scored more than forty films and, at several points during his life, film work was all he could get and he had no choice but to provide music for Communist propaganda reels. For *The Unforgettable Year 1919* (1951), Shostakovich composed *The Assault on Beautiful Gorky*, a romantic Rachmaninov-style piano work that has become a Classic FM favourite. *The Gadfly* (1955) included a haunting *Romance*, later made popular as the theme tune to the TV series *Reilly, Ace of Spies*.

### Sergei Prokofiev (1891–1953)

In 1933, another great Russian composer, Sergei Prokofiev, was approached to write his first film score. He completed the music for *Lieutenant Kijé* (1934) quickly and its Christmassy 'Troika' has remained a favourite. For *Alexander Nevsky* (1938),

Prokofiev studied twelfth- and thirteenth-century church music to try to create an authentic sound for the film but decided that a contemporary approach would suit the action better. *Nevsky*'s director, Sergei Eisenstein, described Prokofiev as 'a perfect composer for the screen'.

## Arthur Honegger (1892–1955)

In France, composer Arthur Honegger wrote more than forty film scores, starting out with music for Abel Gance's *La Roue* (1923), which made use of musical effects suggesting the rhythm of railways. Never afraid to experiment, Honegger even ventured into the world of animation with *L'Idée* (1932) in which he made use of the early electronic instrument, the ondes Martenot.

## Jacques Ibert (1890–1962)

Jacques Ibert also wrote numerous accomplished scores. He originally wanted to be an actor and brought his passion for drama into every medium in which he worked. He stepped in to write the music for *Don Quixote* (1933) when health problems prevented Maurice Ravel from completing the score. Ibert's music for Orson Welles' *Macbeth* (1948) is a mixture of eerie sounds emerging from a selection of exotic percussion, as well as brilliant brass writing for the battles.

### Arthur Benjamin (1893–1960)

Arthur Benjamin studied composition at the Royal College of Music in London under Charles Villiers Stanford before pursuing a career as a piano professor, conductor and composer. He was approached to write his first score, *The Scarlet Pimpernel* (1934), by one of his pupils, Muir Matheson, who had become music director of the London Films Studio. For Hitchcock, Benjamin composed the dramatic *'Storm Cloud Cantata'*, which plays an important part in the climax of *The Man Who Knew Too Much* (1934). Benjamin was among the few early film composers concerned about how the music would actually sound through cinema speakers; he deliberately pared down his orchestration to aim for the clearest possible sound quality.

### Arthur Bliss (1891–1975)

Among the British composers who, for financial reasons, could not turn down an offer from the movies, Arthur Bliss was among the most distinguished.

*Things to Come* (1936), his landmark score, set a new standard for the genre – symphonic in scope and well able to hold its own in the concert hall and on record.

### Arnold Bax (1883–1953)

Film music revived the flagging career of Master of the King's Music Arnold Bax, one of Britain's most sophisticated composers. Just as he was contemplating retirement, an offer came to write for the cinema – a medium in which he had little interest and no experience. His score for *Oliver Twist* (1948) is among Bax's masterpieces, despite the fact that the composer loathed Dickens' book.

### Benjamin Frankel (1906–1973)

Benjamin Frankel gained recognition at the end of the Second World War with some excellent chamber music before becoming reportedly the highest-paid British film composer of the 1950s. He composed eight symphonies, an opera, music for almost seventy films and television programmes, and a violin concerto in memory of the victims of the Holocaust. He was an enthusiast for the serialist style of composition pioneered by Schoenberg and based his acclaimed *Curse of the Werewolf* (1961) score on its principles.

### William Alwyn (1905–1985)

William Alwyn, professor of composition at the Royal Academy of Music for thirty years, wrote music for more than seventy films. He considered himself a late-Romantic composer who nevertheless loved to make use of dissonance when the occasion demanded it. His two most famous scores, *Odd Man Out* (1947) and *The Fallen Idol* (1948), were the fruit of an excellent partnership with director Carol Reed. Alwyn liked *Odd Man Out* so much that he reused its theme in his *First Symphony*.

### Ralph Vaughan Williams (1872–1958)

A giant of twentieth-century British music, Ralph Vaughan Williams ventured into film music with *The 49th Parallel* (1941) starring Laurence Olivier – the story of a stranded U-boat trying to find its way into neutral waters. It demonstrated that the composer was as serious about his film scores as he was about his concert works. His music was always at its most dramatic when it depicted human beings battling against nature. The extraordinary score for

*Scott of the Antarctic* (1948), with its wordless-choir blizzard, organ-blasting glaciers, and evocations of glittering ice floes, was used five years later as the basis for Vaughan Williams' seventh symphony, *Sinfonia Antarctica.*

## William Walton (1902–1983)

William Walton first got involved in films through his association with the director–producer Paul Czinner. He wrote four soundtracks for Czinner, including his first Shakespeare film, *As You Like It* (1936), which also starred Laurence Olivier. After scoring five wartime films, including *The First of the Few* (1942) – from which his popular *Spitfire Prelude and Fugue* was taken – Walton was approached by Olivier to write the music for *Henry V* (1944). The composer was nominated for an Oscar for his brilliantly colourful score, filled with heroic battle music, Renaissance pastiches and pastoral romanticism.

Walton offered Olivier three further scores for *Hamlet* (1948), *Richard III* (1955) and *Three Sisters* (1970). When his thrilling music for *The Battle of Britain* (1969) was dropped in favour of a score by Ron Goodwin, Olivier – who was appearing in the

film – threatened to remove his name from the credits unless Walton's music was included. As a result,
some of Walton's score was reinstated.

### Malcolm Arnold (1921–2006)

Few British composers in the twentieth century
were more versatile than Malcolm Arnold. He
wrote the music for dozens of films, including the
award-winning *Bridge on the River Kwai* (1957)
and *The Inn of the Sixth Happiness* (1958). Arnold
loved working on soundtracks, describing it as
'immensely liberating'. For *Kwai*, he wrote all of
the music in less than two weeks. The speed at
which he composed and his natural gift for orchestration and melody made him an ideal collaborator
for directors.

### Richard Rodney Bennett (1936–2012)

Richard Rodney Bennett was another British
composer who excelled across musical genres.
Rigorously trained in the modernist style, Bennett
composed some fifty scores. He received Oscar
nominations for *Far from the Madding Crowd*
(1967), *Nicholas and Alexandra* (1971) and *Mur-
der on the Orient Express* (1974), which has a

marvellous waltz theme that takes off and powers along like the eponymous steam train.

## Michael Nyman (born in 1944)

As an academic writer about music, it was Michael Nyman who first coined the term 'minimalism' in relation to the style of music built on subtly shifting, repetitive patterns. The genre served Nyman well in his own squawking, highly rhythmic scores for Peter Greenaway's films, including *The Draughtsman's Contract* (1982). In 1993, Nyman's sensuous, folk-inspired music for *The Piano* (1993) was a huge commercial success, selling more than three million copies worldwide.

## Aaron Copland (1900–1990)

There are few film composers – particularly for Westerns – who have not been influenced by the movie scores and cowboy ballets of Aaron Copland. Copland developed a distinctively American sound that lent itself well to movies about life in small towns and rural areas. His first major movie success was the music to *Of Mice and Men* (1939) – a formula that was repeated with *The Red Pony* (1949), also an adaptation of a John Steinbeck novel. Scoring just eight movies, Copland won an Oscar for *The Heiress* (1949), based on the novel *Washington Square* by Henry James.

## Leonard Bernstein (1918–1990)

One of the most influential and talented of American musicians, Leonard Bernstein wrote just one film score but left his mark on the whole of the twentieth century. Bernstein was a polymath – a pianist, conductor, educator, showman, writer of musicals, symphonies and operas. His only film score, *On the Waterfront* (1954), is at once tense, dramatic and lyrical, featuring all the trademark rhythms and harmonies that would become so familiar in Bernstein's masterpiece, the musical *West Side Story* (1961).

## Philip Glass (born in 1937)

One of the most popular of today's American classical composers, Philip Glass has combined his film work with numerous operas, concert works and popular albums. *Koyaanisqatsi* (1983) is a unique piece of cinema, perfectly combining Glass's music with powerful images of rural and urban America. His hypnotic and repetitive works are considered by some to be indistinguishable from one another but, nevertheless, they have made an effective contribution to many films, including *The Hours* (2002), *The Illusionist* (2006) and *Notes on a Scandal* (2006).

## Cinematic Lives of the Great Composers

The lives of the great classical composers have often provided fascinating subject matter for movies, although, on most occasions, there has been little resemblance between the actual facts of a composer's life and his story on screen.

Starting in the 1940s, 'biopics' of great composers, in which classical music was fully integrated into the films' soundtracks, became extremely popular. At the same time, other dramas centred around a leading character who was a musician – for example, *Humoresque* (1946), starring Joan Crawford.

The always controversial British director Ken Russell did much to bring the music of the great composers to filmgoers' attention, while playing fast and loose with the facts and adding fantasy elements that are distinctly his own. After producing exquisite short films for BBC Television about, among others,

Elgar, Bartók, Delius, Debussy and Richard Strauss, Russell turned his attention to vivid adaptations of D. H. Lawrence novels and outrageous composer biopics, covering the lives of Mahler, Tchaikovsky and Liszt. A fan of great soundtracks himself, Russell presented a series on film music, *Ken Russell's Movie Classics*, on Classic FM in the mid-1990s.

Here is a list of some great composers who have been portrayed on screen and the actors who played them in some of the more interesting cinematic versions of their lives:

Ludwig van Beethoven: played by Gary Oldman in *Immortal Beloved* (1995) and Ed Harris in *Copying Beethoven* (2006).

Hector Berlioz: played by Jean-Louis Barrault in *La Symphonie fantastique* (1942).

Frédéric Chopin: played by Cornel Wilde in *A Song to Remember* (1945) and Hugh Grant in *Impromptu* (1991).

George Gershwin: played by Robert Alda in *Rhapsody in Blue* (1945).

Gilbert and Sullivan: played by Nigel Bruce and Claud Allister in *Lillian Russell* (1940), Robert Morley and Maurice Evans in *The Story of*

*Gilbert and Sullivan* (1953) and Jim Broadbent and Allan Corduner in *Topsy Turvy* (1999).

Edvard Grieg: played by Toralv Maurstad in *Song of Norway* (1970).

Georg Frideric Handel: played by Wilfred Lawson in *The Great Mr Handel* (1942).

Franz Liszt: played by Dirk Bogarde in *Song Without End* (1960) and Roger Daltrey in *Lisztomania* (1975).

Gustav Mahler: played by Robert Powell in *Mahler* (1974).

Wolfgang Amadeus Mozart: played by Tom Hulce in *Amadeus* (1984).

Niccolò Paganini: played by Stewart Granger in *The Magic Bow* (1946) and David Garrett in *The Devil's Violinist* (2013).

Robert Schumann: played by Paul Henreid in *Song of Love* (1947).

Dmitri Shostakovich: played by Ben Kingsley in *Testimony* (1988).

Johann Strauss II: played by Kerwin Mathews in *The Waltz King* (1963) and Horst Buchholz in *The Great Waltz* (1972).

Pyotr Ilyich Tchaikovsky: played by Frank Sundstrom in *Song of My Heart* (1947) and Richard Chamberlain in *The Music Lovers* (1970).

Richard Wagner: played by Alan Badel in *Magic Fire* (1955), Trevor Howard in *Ludwig* (1972), Paul Nicholas in *Lisztomania* (1975) and Richard Burton in *Wagner* (1983).

More composers are portrayed in the Italian film *Casa Ricordi* (1954) than in any other movie. The film tells the story of the legendary music-publishing family, the Ricordis. The soundtrack featured the voices of some of the great opera singers of the day, including Tito Gobbi, Renata Tebaldi and Mario del Monaco.

## 20 Classical Pieces Featured in Films

The popularity of certain great classical works has been completely revitalised by their use in a movie. Here are twenty that have become favourites after their inclusion in box-office hits.

| | |
|---|---|
| *2001: A Space Odyssey* | Richard Strauss: *Also Sprach Zarathustra: Sunrise* |
| *Apocalypse Now* | Wagner: *Die Walküre: Ride of the Valkyries* |
| *Babe* | Saint-Saëns: *Organ Symphony* (finale) |
| *Brief Encounter* | Rachmaninov: *Piano Concerto No. 2* |

# Classical Composers at the Movies

| | |
|---|---|
| *Chariots of Fire* | Allegri: *Miserere* |
| *A Clockwork Orange* | Beethoven: *Symphony No. 9: 'Ode to Joy'* |
| *Death in Venice* | Mahler: *Symphony No. 5: Adagietto* (4th movement) |
| *Diva* | Catalani: *La Wally: 'Ebben? Ne andrò lontana'* |
| *Driving Miss Daisy* | Dvořák: *Rusalka: Song to the Moon* |
| *Elvira Madigan* | Mozart: *Piano Concerto No. 21 in C: Andante* (2nd movement) |
| *Excalibur* | Orff: *Carmina Burana: 'O Fortuna'* |
| *Fantasia* | Dukas: *The Sorcerer's Apprentice* |
| *Life is Beautiful* | Offenbach: *The Tales of Hoffmann:* Barcarolle |
| *The Madness of King George* | Handel: *Zadok the Priest* |
| *Moonstruck* | Puccini: *La bohème: 'Che gelida manina'* |
| *Out of Africa* | Mozart: *Clarinet Concerto in A: Adagio* (2nd movement) |
| *Platoon* | Barber: *Adagio for Strings* |
| *Raging Bull* | Mascagni: *Cavalleria rusticana: Intermezzo* |
| *A Room with a View* | Puccini: *Gianni Schicchi: 'O mio babbino caro'* |
| *The Shawshank Redemption* | Mozart: *The Marriage of Figaro: 'Sull'aria'* |

## *Carmen* **on Screen**

Bizet's opera *Carmen* has always fascinated film-makers, inspiring more than seventy films, including some forty silent-movie versions. Cecil B. DeMille cast Metropolitan Opera star Geraldine Farrar in the 1915 version, although not a single noise was heard coming out of her. Carmen has also been played by such luminaries as Theda Bara in *Carmen* (1915), Dolores del Rio in *The Loves of Carmen* (1927), Rita Hayworth in *The Loves of Carmen* (1948), and Beyoncé in *Carmen: A Hip Hopera* (2001). In Charlie Chaplin's *Burlesque on Carmen* (1916), Don José is reinvented as 'Darn Hosiery'. In the all-black *Carmen Jones* (1954), Dorothy Dandridge's singing part was dubbed by a nineteen-year-old music student called Marilyn Horne who was paid $300 for her role. Horne went on to become one of the greatest opera stars of the post-war period. A 1983 flamenco version by Carlos Saura was a big success, while *U-Carmen eKhayelitsha* (2005) set the opera in a modern-day South African township. In *Babe* (1995), the story of a pig that wants to be a sheepdog, a trio of mice sings the *Toreador Song*.

*eight*

# That's All, Folks!

Whether it's a hippo in a tutu pirouetting to Ponchielli's *Dance of the Hours* in *Fantasia*, Elmer Fudd chasing Bugs Bunny across mountaintops rasping 'Kill da Wabbit' to the tune of Wagner's *Ride of the Valkyries* in *What's Opera, Doc?* or Randy Newman singing *'You've Got a Friend in Me'* over the opening credits of *Toy Story*, there's no doubt that music and animation have been happy bedfellows since the earliest days of cinema.

As far back as 1919, the Fleischer brothers – whose studio put Betty Boop and Popeye on screen – had worked with a basic process for adding sound to film. They also invented the bouncing ball over lyrics to 'sing-along' films to help audiences keep in time with the music pumping out of the cinema's organ.

The Fleischers' *My Old Kentucky Home* in 1926 was probably the first sound cartoon. But Max Fleischer didn't believe sound would catch on and held back, allowing Walt Disney to steal the brothers' thunder.

Everything changed with the release of *The Jazz Singer* (1927) and the arrival of the 'talkies'. Animation studios were among the first to explore the possibilities of sound. For *Steamboat Willie* (1928), his third short starring Mickey Mouse, Walt Disney added an original score and sound effects. The cartoon got a better reception than the main feature.

### Carl Stalling (1891–1972)

Stalling has been called the twentieth century's most famous unknown composer. He wrote the scores for literally hundreds of animated shorts. Anyone who has ever watched a *Looney Tunes* cartoon will have heard his fiendishly clever, frenetic music. Stalling was working as an organist in Kansas City when he was recruited by Walt Disney to be his musical director. As sound took off, Stalling suggested that Disney launch a series of shorts that would tell their stories through music. The *Silly Symphonies* series began with *The Skeleton Dance* (1929). Stalling left Disney in 1930 and later joined Warner Brothers where he averaged one score a week for more than two decades. He was the master of the musical joke, shamelessly referencing and playing with classical pieces and popular song tunes. *A Corny Concerto* (1943) – in which Bugs Bunny and Porky Pig perform a ballet – and *The Rabbit of Seville* (1950) are among his masterpieces.

## Alan Menken (born in 1949)

After a fallow period in the 1970s and 1980s, Disney's cartoon-feature output was re-animated with a succession of musical spectaculars penned by Alan Menken. After meeting lyricist Howard Ashman at a musical theatre workshop, the pair had a stage and screen hit with *Little Shop of Horrors*. With Disney's return to lavish features, Menken's and Ashman's *The Little Mermaid* (1989) became the highest grossing animated film up to that point. *Beauty and the Beast* (1991) became the first animated feature to receive a Best Picture nomination at the Oscars. Ashman wrote several lyrics for *Aladdin* (1992) before his untimely death. Menken completed the score with British lyricist Tim Rice. Menken went on to work with Broadway tunesmith Stephen Schwartz on *Pocahontas* (1995) and *The Hunchback of Notre Dame* (1996). Menken has continued his working relationship with

Disney on *Hercules* (1997), *Home on the Range* (2004), *Enchanted* (2007) and *Tangled* (2010).

With the emergence of brilliant young talent all over the world, animation has enjoyed a new lease of life in the past two decades as one of cinema's most lucrative genres. The increasing sophistication of computer-generated animation has seen a proliferation of highly entertaining family films – from the likes of Disney–Pixar and DreamWorks – while the British-based Aardman Animations revived stop-motion animation to universal adulation with their Wallace and Gromit films (1989–2008) and *Chicken Run* (2000). From Hans Zimmer's stable, Harry Gregson-Williams (born in 1961) and John Powell (born in 1963) have emerged with a particular talent for writing music for animated features, producing excellent scores for *Chicken Run* and the *Shrek* series (2001–2010).

## Classics and Cartoons

While you might be thinking that Disney's *Fantasia* (1940) was the first animated film to match hand-drawn images with classical music, it was in fact as far back as 1928 that the pioneering silhouette animator Lotte Reiniger was working with such musical giants as Paul Hindemith and Kurt Weill on a feature-length version of *Dr Dolittle*. Another of Reiniger's projects was an animated version of Ravel's *L'Enfant et les sortilèges*.

As animation techniques became more sophisticated, cartoonists found classical music to be a good source of inspiration as well as a prime target for their gags. In Mickey Mouse's first colour cartoon, *The Band Concert* (1935), Mickey's best attempts to get his band through a performance of Rossini's Overture to *William Tell* are disrupted by Donald Duck noisily selling popcorn and playing 'Turkey in the Straw' on his flute.

As the duck's popularity overtook that of the mouse, Disney dreamed up the idea of reviving Mickey's career with a starring role in a short based on *The Sorcerer's Apprentice* by the French composer Paul Dukas. With the involvement of the Philadelphia Orchestra's conductor, Leopold Stokowski, the short grew into the much more ambitious *Fantasia*, a full-length animated feature taking the form of a concert of favourite pieces, brought alive with stunning visual sequences by Disney animators. Ever the innovator, Disney even developed an ambitious sound system for *Fantasia* using seven tracks and thirty loudspeakers.

Some of *Fantasia*'s sequences work better than

others but the beauty of the animation, its wit and ingenuity, has hardly been bettered. Disney's hope that new segments could be inserted into *Fantasia* from time to time was finally realised with *Fantasia 2000*, a less successful venture but nevertheless featuring some spectacular moments – including a stylised, loosely drawn *Rhapsody in Blue* and a magical interpretation of Stravinsky's *The Firebird*.

In 1943, Warner Brothers took a swipe at *Fantasia* with *A Corny Concerto*, sending up Johann Strauss II's *Blue Danube* and Disney's *The Ugly Duckling*, with a black baby duck fighting off a buzzard. The Italian animator Bruno Bozzetto (born in 1938) also sent up *Fantasia* in *Allegro non troppo* (1976). Bozzetto's segments, though, are more than a parody. Its six sequences, including those based on Ravel's *Boléro* and Sibelius's *Valse Triste* are exceptional in their own right.

In the Tom and Jerry short *The Cat Concerto* (1947), Tom tries to perform Liszt's *Hungarian Rhapsody No. 2* while Jerry is determined to enjoy his sleep inside the piano. In *Baton Bunny* (1959), Bugs Bunny attempts to conduct an orchestra in *Morning, Noon and Night in Vienna* by Franz von Suppé, while fighting off an annoying fly. In 1960, Chuck Jones made *High Note* in which the sheet music for *The*

*Blue Danube* is constructed on the musical stave by a cast of animated notes and symbols.

## What's Opera, Doc?

Of all classical music forms, however, opera has best fed the imagination of Hollywood's greatest animators, with *The Barber of Seville* and the sextet from Donizetti's *Lucia di Lammermoor* popping up most frequently in cartoon classics.

Bugs Bunny's first foray into opera was *Long-Haired Hare* (1949), which features the *Barber* aria *'Largo al factotum'*. The following year, *The Rabbit of Seville* saw Bugs playing the barber to his tormented customer, Elmer Fudd. Woody Woodpecker also tried his hand at opera and hairdressing in *The Barber of Seville* (1944). In *Notes to You* (1941), Porky Pig is kept awake at night by an alley cat howling *'Largo al factotum'*. After Porky shoots the cat, a chorus of ghostly felines arrives to sing the *Lucia* sextet. The cartoon was remade in 1948 with Elmer Fudd and Sylvester. Tex Avery's *The Magical Maestro* (1952) tells the story of a man trying to sing *The Barber of Seville* as a magician persists in transforming his costumes. In Disney's *The Whale Who Wanted to Sing at the Met* (1946), Nelson Eddy voiced Willie the whale who can sing tenor, baritone and bass at the same time. Willie dreams of auditioning with '*Largo al factotum*' and the *Lucia* sextet before singing *Pagliacci* at the Met, with the 'motley' on (the costume of a court jester), his whale tears requiring the audience to put up umbrellas.

The Disney studio also brought the ultimate diva to cinema screens – Clara Cluck, a full-bodied and not particularly talented chicken, voiced by singer Florence Gill. Clara Cluck sang Juliet to Donald Duck's Romeo in *Mickey's Grand Opera* (1936) and gobbled her way single-handedly through the *Lucia* sextet in *The Orphan's Benefit* (1934).

Animation's finest opera moment by far was *What's Opera, Doc?* (1957) in which Wagner's *Ring* is compressed into just six minutes. Elmer Fudd in armour chases Bugs Bunny across mountains, intoning 'Kill da wabbit, kill da wabbit' to the tune of the *Ride of the Valkyries*. Even Pablo Picasso is said to have admired the artistry of *What's Opera, Doc?*

Other cartoon characters encountering opera included Mr Magoo, stumbling his way chaotically through an opera in *Stage Door Magoo* (1955), magpies Heckle and Jeckle in *Off to the Opera* (1952) and Gandy Goose in *Carmen's Veranda* (1944).

# nine

# And the Winner Is ...

The Academy Awards – or Oscars – presented each year in Los Angeles by the Academy of Motion Picture Arts and Sciences are the most prestigious, coveted and eagerly anticipated of all movie awards. The first Oscars ceremony was held in 1929, although the award for musical scoring was not established until 1934. At various points in the Oscars' history, there have been two awards for music – at times one for scoring and one for adaptation (of a stage musical, for example). In other years, Oscars have been given for dramatic score and for musical or comedy score. For the purposes of this table, we have limited the listing to those awards given for music especially composed for films rather than adaptations of stage shows or songs.

The British Academy of Film and Television Awards, or BAFTAs, have risen in prestige over the years and are now considered to be the British equivalent of the Oscars. They began in 1938 but presentation of an award for film music commenced only in 1968.

| Year | Oscar | BAFTA |
|------|-------|-------|
| 1934 | Victor Schertziner and Gus Kahn<br>*One Night of Love* | |
| 1935 | Max Steiner<br>*The Informer* | |
| 1936 | Erich Wolfgang Korngold<br>*Anthony Adverse* | |
| 1937 | Charles Previn<br>*100 Men and a Girl* | |
| 1938 | Erich Wolfgang Korngold<br>*The Adventures of Robin Hood* | |
| 1939 | Richard Hageman et al.<br>*Stagecoach* | |
| 1940 | Alfred Newman<br>*Tin Pan Alley* | |
| 1941 | Bernard Herrmann<br>*All that Money Can Buy* | |
| 1942 | Max Steiner<br>*Now, Voyager* | |

| Year | Oscar | BAFTA |
|------|-------|-------|
| 1943 | Alfred Newman *The Song of Bernadette* | |
| 1944 | Max Steiner *Since You Went Away* | |
| 1945 | Miklós Rózsa *Spellbound* | |
| 1946 | Hugo Friedhofer *The Best Years of Our Lives* | |
| 1947 | Miklós Rózsa *A Double Life* | |
| 1948 | Brian Easdale *The Red Shoes* | |
| 1949 | Aaron Copland *The Heiress* | |
| 1950 | Franz Waxman *Sunset Boulevard* | |
| 1951 | Franz Waxman *A Place in the Sun* | |
| 1952 | Dimitri Tiomkin *High Noon* | |
| 1953 | Bronislau Kaper *Lili* | |
| 1954 | Dimitri Tiomkin *The High and the Mighty* | |
| 1955 | Alfred Newman *Love is a Many-Splendored Thing* | |

| Year | Oscar | BAFTA |
|---|---|---|
| 1956 | Victor Young<br>*Around the World in Eighty Days* | |
| 1957 | Malcolm Arnold<br>*The Bridge on the River Kwai* | |
| 1958 | Dimitri Tiomkin<br>*The Old Man and the Sea* | |
| 1959 | Miklós Rósza<br>*Ben-Hur* | |
| 1960 | Ernest Gold<br>*Exodus* | |
| 1961 | Henry Mancini<br>*Breakfast at Tiffany's* | |
| 1962 | Maurice Jarre<br>*Lawrence of Arabia* | |
| 1963 | John Addison<br>*Tom Jones* | |
| 1964 | Richard M. & Robert B. Sherman<br>*Mary Poppins* | |
| 1965 | Maurice Jarre<br>*Doctor Zhivago* | |
| 1966 | John Barry<br>*Born Free* | |
| 1967 | Elmer Bernstein<br>*Thoroughly Modern Millie* | |
| 1968 | John Barry<br>*The Lion in Winter* | John Barry<br>*The Lion in Winter* |

| Year | Oscar | BAFTA |
|------|-------|-------|
| 1969 | Burt Bacharach<br>*Butch Cassidy and the Sundance Kid* | Mikis Thedorakis<br>*Z* |
| 1970 | Francis Lai<br>*Love Story* | Burt Bacharach<br>*Butch Cassidy and the Sundance Kid* |
| 1971 | Michel Legrand<br>*Summer of '42* | Michel Legrand<br>*Summer of '42* |
| 1972 | Charles Chaplin et al.<br>*Limelight* | Nino Rota<br>*The Godfather* |
| 1973 | Marvin Hamlisch<br>*The Way We Were* | Alan Price<br>*O Lucky Man!* |
| 1974 | Nino Rota and Carmine Coppola<br>*The Godfather Part II* | Richard Rodney Bennett<br>*Murder on the Orient Express* |
| 1975 | John Williams<br>*Jaws* | John Williams<br>*Jaws/The Towering Inferno* |
| 1976 | Jerry Goldsmith<br>*The Omen* | Bernard Herrmann<br>*Taxi Driver* |
| 1977 | Jonathan Tunick<br>*A Little Night Music* | John Addison<br>*A Bridge too Far* |
| 1978 | Giorgio Moroder<br>*Midnight Express* | John Williams<br>*Star Wars* |
| 1979 | Georges Delerue<br>*A Little Romance* | Ennio Morricone<br>*Days of Heaven* |
| 1980 | Michael Gore<br>*Fame* | John Williams<br>*The Empire Strikes Back* |

| Year | Oscar | BAFTA |
|------|-------|-------|
| 1981 | Vangelis<br>*Chariots of Fire* | Carl Davis<br>*The French Lieutenant's Woman* |
| 1982 | John Williams<br>*E.T.* | John Williams<br>*E.T.* |
| 1983 | Bill Conti<br>*The Right Stuff* | Ryuichi Sakamoto<br>*Merry Christmas, Mr Lawrence* |
| 1984 | Maurice Jarre<br>*A Passage to India* | Ennio Morricone<br>*Once Upon a Time in America* |
| 1985 | John Barry<br>*Out of Africa* | Maurice Jarre<br>*Witness* |
| 1986 | Herbie Hancock<br>*Round Midnight* | Ennio Morricone<br>*The Mission* |
| 1987 | Ryuichi Sakamoto and David Byrne<br>*The Last Emperor* | Ennio Morricone<br>*The Untouchables* |
| 1988 | Dave Grusin<br>*The Milagro Beanfield War* | John Williams<br>*Empire of the Sun* |
| 1989 | Alan Menken<br>*The Little Mermaid* | Maurice Jarre<br>*Dead Poets Society* |
| 1990 | John Barry<br>*Dances with Wolves* | Ennio and Andreas Morricone<br>*Nuovo Cinema Paradiso* |
| 1991 | Alan Menken<br>*Beauty and the Beast* | Jean-Claude Petit<br>*Cyrano de Bergerac* |
| 1992 | Alan Menken<br>*Aladdin* | David Hirschfelder<br>*Strictly Ballroom* |

| Year | Oscar | BAFTA |
|------|-------|-------|
| 1993 | John Williams<br>*Schindler's List* | John Williams<br>*Schindler's List* |
| 1994 | Hans Zimmer<br>*The Lion King* | Don Was<br>*Backbeat* |
| 1995 | Luis Enriques Bacalov<br>*Il Postino* | Luis Enriques Bacalov<br>*Il Postino* |
| 1996 | Gabriel Yared<br>*The English Patient* | Gabriel Yared<br>*The English Patient* |
| 1997 | James Horner<br>*Titanic* | Nellee Hooper and<br>Craig Armstrong<br>*William Shakespeare's<br>Romeo + Juliet* |
| 1998 | Nicola Piovani<br>*Life is Beautiful* | David Hirschfelder<br>*Elizabeth* |
| 1999 | John Corigliano<br>*The Red Violin* | Thomas Newman<br>*American Beauty* |
| 2000 | Tan Dun<br>*Crouching Tiger,<br>Hidden Dragon* | Tan Dun<br>*Crouching Tiger,<br>Hidden Dragon* |
| 2001 | Howard Shore<br>*The Lord of the Rings:<br>The Fellowship of the Ring* | Craig Armstrong and<br>Marius De Vries<br>*Moulin Rouge* |
| 2002 | Elliot Goldenthal<br>*Frida* | Philip Glass<br>*The Hours* |
| 2003 | Howard Shore<br>*The Lord of the Rings:<br>The Return of the King* | Gabriel Yared and<br>T-Bone Burnett<br>*Cold Mountain* |
| 2004 | Jan A. P. Kaczmarek<br>*Finding Neverland* | Gustavo Santaolalla<br>*The Motorcycle Diaries* |

| Year | Oscar | BAFTA |
|------|-------|-------|
| 2005 | Gustavo Santaolalla<br>*Brokeback Mountain* | John Williams<br>*Memoirs of a Geisha* |
| 2006 | Gustavo Santaolalla<br>*Babel* | Gustavo Santaolalla<br>*Babel* |
| 2007 | Dario Marianelli<br>*Atonement* | Christopher Gunning<br>*La vie en rose* |
| 2008 | A. R. Rahman<br>*Slumdog Millionaire* | A. R. Rahman<br>*Slumdog Millionaire* |
| 2009 | Michael Giacchino<br>*Up* | Michael Giacchino<br>*Up* |
| 2010 | Trent Reznor and<br>Atticus Ross<br>*The Social Network* | Alexandre Desplat<br>*The King's Speech* |
| 2011 | Ludovico Bource<br>*The Artist* | Ludovico Bource<br>*The Artist* |
| 2012 | Mychael Danna<br>*Life of Pi* | Thomas Newman<br>*Skyfall* |
| 2013 | Steven Price<br>*Gravity* | Steven Price<br>*Gravity* |

# ten

# The Top 30 Film Themes to Download

Here's a list of thirty tracks that represent the most popular film music ever written. You can find them as a downloadable playlist on our website at: ClassicFM.com/handyguides.

### 1. Howard Shore: *The Lord of the Rings* (2001–3)

Canadian Shore was an unusual choice for the most ambitious production in film history – but he triumphed. Nothing in recent years comes close for scale, drama, melody and skill.

### 2. Hans Zimmer and Lisa Gerrard: *Gladiator* (2000)

An Oscar-nominated score for the epic that revived the swords and sandals blockbuster. Gerrard's haunting voice adds a timeless quality to Zimmer's atmospheric music.

### 3. John Williams: *Schindler's List* (1993)

Based on a heart-rending violin melody, Williams' score captures the traditions and plight of Eastern Europe's Jewry – and the pity of man's inhumanity to man.

### 4. John Williams: *Star Wars* (1977)

Williams' brilliant music for the sci-fi classic revived the golden age of Hollywood film music, when grand symphonic scores were the order of the day.

### 5. John Barry: *Dances with Wolves* (1990)

Reflecting the movie's political and ecological themes, Barry rejected the usual Western clichés for a gentle depiction of a vast, beautiful landscape. Kevin Costner directed and starred in the film.

### 6. John Barry: *Out of Africa* (1985)

Barry's winning score reflects the expansiveness of the landscape and acts as a backdrop to Meryl Streep's and Robert Redford's doomed love story.

Mozart's *Clarinet Concerto* also meanders over the bush from an old gramophone.

### 7. Klaus Badelt: *Pirates of the Caribbean* (2003)

Hans Zimmer's protégé Badelt pulled out all the stops for the swaggering antics of Captain Jack Sparrow on the high seas. Thrilling, surging and just a little bit cheeky.

### 8. Vangelis: *Chariots of Fire* (1981)

A seminal synthesizer soundtrack that has lived on beyond its original purpose, to accompany sporting events and broadcasts. Perfect for jogging to. The film won four Oscars including one for Best Original Score.

### 9. John Williams: *Jurassic Park* (1993)

Williams always captures and complements the sense of wonder that Spielberg creates on screen. The theme here is a sweeping, stirring anthem.

### 10. Ennio Morricone: *The Mission* (1986)

Two decades after his Spaghetti-Western heyday, Morricone created his best-loved score, skilfully mixing Amazonian rhythms with the Baroque style of *The Mission*'s Jesuit missionaries.

### 11. Elmer Bernstein: *The Magnificent Seven* (1960)

The greatest Western theme ever, as Bernstein draws on Copland's Wild West ballets, creating a galloping, expansive romp that has remained a worldwide favourite. The film starred Yul Brynner, Steve McQueen and Charles Bronson.

### 12. John Williams: *Harry Potter and the Philosopher's Stone* (2001)

J. K. Rowling's first big-screen blockbuster introduced us to Daniel Radcliffe, Rupert Grint and Emma Watson, as well as Williams' leaping, mysterious themes.

### 13. Nigel Hess: *Ladies in Lavender* (2004)

Star violinist Joshua Bell played Hess's touching theme for Maggie Smith and Judi Dench as spinster sisters in Cornwall. Massenet and Debussy also featured.

### 14. John Williams: *Saving Private Ryan* (1998)

The stirring *Hymn to the Fallen* has become an

essential Classic FM track and the perfect accompaniment to solemn ceremonies.

### 15. Michael Nyman: *The Piano* (1993)

This simple, haunting score still continues to capture hearts. Nyman's music is critical to the plot of *The Piano*; it's the only voice the heroine has to communicate with.

### 16. Maurice Jarre: *Lawrence of Arabia* (1962)

The famous theme immediately whisks you away to expanses of sand and blazing heat. Maurice Jarre's score evokes the romance of the desert.

### 17. Maurice Jarre: *Dr Zhivago* (1965)

The best film themes recreate the movie's visual imagery. Jarre's partnership with director David Lean created a stupendous, swirling, snowy soundscape.

### 18. John Williams: *Raiders of the Lost Ark* (1981)

Williams created a blistering march for the hero Indiana Jones. It conjures up the world of high adventure and helped launch a franchise that looks set to continue.

## 19. John Williams: *E.T.* (1982)

It's impossible to imagine the lovable alien and his friends swooping through the night sky on their bikes without hearing Williams' soaring music.

## 20. Max Steiner: *Gone with the Wind* (1939)

Steiner wrote three hours of music in just three months while also working on other movies. The stirring backdrop to this film became his most popular work.

## 21. James Horner: *Braveheart* (1995)

Horner's music is about as authentically Scottish as Mel Gibson's take on the thirteenth-century patriot. But as a soundtrack it's wonderfully uplifting.

## 22. James Horner: *Titanic* (1997)

Another soundtrack from Horner – this one with incongruous electronic instruments and Celine Dion's famous belter of a ballad, which sold millions.

## 23. Jerome Moross: *The Big Country* (1958)

In his handful of scores, Moross perfected an exciting rugged style inspired by his first experience of the Great Plains. An influential Western soundtrack.

## 24. Trevor Jones and Randy Edelman: *The Last of the Mohicans* (1992)

Star Daniel Day-Lewis had little to say, but the music spoke volumes. A majestic and thrilling soundtrack.

## 25. Ron Goodwin: *633 Squadron* (1964)

One of British cinema's catchiest themes: gung-ho heroism and wartime bravery, set to a rhythm that echoes the squadron number.

## 26. Stanley Myers: *The Deer Hunter* (1978)

Myers' guitar piece *Cavatina*, performed by the other John Williams, was the stand-out moment from this disturbing drama about Vietnam veterans.

## 27. Richard Addinsell: *Dangerous Moonlight* (1941)

Second World War drama about a pianist trying to recover his memory. Addinsell's cod-Rachmaninov *Warsaw Concerto* remains hugely popular.

## 28. Thomas Newman: *American Beauty* (1999)

Newman's sparse and icy score gave Sam Mendes' portrait of a dysfunctional family its uneasy edge.

The film starred Kevin Spacey as a man in midlife crisis.

## 29. Vangelis: *Blade Runner* (1982)

Ridley Scott's futuristic thriller was given the full electronic treatment by Greece's keyboard wizard, with added saxophone for raw emotion.

## 30. Nino Rota: *The Godfather* (1972)

Rota was a veteran of film, opera and ballet before he had his biggest hit with *The Godfather*'s love theme. But he had to wait for the sequel to win his Oscar.

# Where To Find
# Out More

If this Handy Guide has whetted your appetite to find out more about film music, one of the best ways to do so is to tune in to Classic FM to hear more of your favourite movie themes. We proudly showcase film music every day in our programmes and, specifically, every Saturday night we have *Saturday Night at the Movies*, featuring the greatest soundtracks, exciting new releases and the world's favourite classical pieces as heard in the movies. And you can find out much more about film music by visiting the dedicated section of our website: ClassicFM.com/discover/filmmusic.

If you would like to delve deeper into the world of film music and its composers, then here is a list of helpful online resource that can assist you on your way.

## Useful Online Resources

| | |
|---|---|
| Film Score Monthly | www.filmscoremonthly.com |
| Film Tracks | www.filmtracks.com |
| Internet Movie Database | www.imdb.com |
| Moviescore Media | www.moviescoremedia.com |
| Music from the Movies | www.musicfromthemovies.com |
| Soundtrack Collector | www.soundtrackcollector.com |
| Soundtrack Net | www.soundtrack.net |
| Stage and Screen Online | www.stageandscreenonline.com |
| Tracksounds | www.tracksounds.com |

## Composer Official and Fan Sites

| | |
|---|---|
| Craig Armstrong | www.craigarmstrongonline.com |
| John Barry | www.johnbarry.org.uk |
| Elmer Bernstein | www.elmerbernstein.com |
| Michael Giacchino | www.michaelgiacchinomusic.com |
| Jerry Goldsmith | www.jerrygoldsmithonline.com |
| Bernard Herrmann | www.bernardherrmann.org |
| James Horner | http://jameshorner-filmmusic.com |
| Michael Kamen | www.michaelkamen.com |
| Erich Wolfgang Korngold | www.korngold-society.org |
| Ennio Morricone | www.enniomorricone.it |
| Howard Shore | www.howardshore.com |
| Franz Waxman | www.franzwaxman.com |
| John Williams | www.jwfan.com |
| Debbie Wiseman | www.debbiewiseman.co.uk |
| Hans Zimmer | www.hans-zimmer.com |

# About Classic FM

If this series of books has whetted your appetite to find out more, one of the best ways to discover what you like about classical music is to listen to Classic FM. We broadcast a huge breadth of classical music 24 hours a day across the UK on 100–102 FM, on DAB digital radio, online at ClassicFM.com, on Sky Channel 0106, on Virgin Media channel 922 and on FreeSat channel 721. You can also download the free Classic FM App, which will enable you to listen to Classic FM on your iPhone, iPod, iPad, Blackberry or Android device.

As well as being able to listen online, you will find a host of interactive features about classical music, composers and musicians on our website, ClassicFM.com. When we first turned on Classic FM's transmitters more than two decades ago, we changed the face of classical music radio in the UK for ever. Now, we are doing the same online.

The very best way to find out more about which pieces of classical music you like is by going out and hearing a live performance by one of our great British orchestras for yourself. There is simply no substitute for seeing the whites of the eyes of a talented soloist as he or she performs a masterpiece on stage only a few feet in front of you, alongside a range of hugely accomplished musicians playing together as one.

Classic FM has a series of partnerships with orchestras across the country: the Bournemouth Symphony Orchestra, the London Symphony Orchestra, the Orchestra of Opera North, the Philharmonia Orchestra, the Royal Liverpool Philharmonic Orchestra, the Royal Northern Sinfonia and the Royal Scottish National Orchestra. And don't forget the brilliant young musicians of the National Children's Orchestra of Great Britain and of the National Youth Orchestra of Great Britain. To see if any of these orchestras have a concert coming up near you, log onto our website at ClassicFM. com and click on the 'Concerts and Events' section. It will also include many other classical concerts – both professional and amateur – that are taking place near where you live.

Happy listening!

# About the Author

Rob Weinberg is the On Air Editor of Classic FM Interactive, the online platform of Global Radio's national classical music station, Classic FM. After graduating with a degree in Expressive Arts from Brighton Polytechnic in 1987, Rob began his career in local radio newsrooms around the UK. He joined Classic FM as a Producer in 1994. Among his proudest achievements are producing Classic FM's six-part centenary series on William Walton with Humphrey Burton; the exclusive UK broadcast of *The Three Tenors at Wembley*; *Ken Russell's Movie Classics*; *The Muppets' Classic Christmas*, presented by Kermit the Frog; *Music – A Joy for Life* with Sir Edward Heath; the first performance at the Royal Albert Hall of Paul McCartney's *Standing Stone*, and the world premiere of Walt Disney Pictures' *Fantasia 2000*. He produced Classic FM's film music show from 1997 to 2007.

# Index

# Index

*In the same series*